EARS THAT HEAR

BY
PATRICIA KING

Published by XP Publishing
A department of Christian Services Association
P.O. Box 1017, Maricopa, Arizona 85139
www.XPpublishing.com

ISBN-13: 978-1-936101-27-6
ISBN-10: 1-936101-27-0

Printed in Canada. For worldwide distribution.

EARS THAT HEAR

Dedicated to

.

Mary Goddard

Who taught me how to discern the voice of God

TABLE OF CONTENTS

FOREWORD
BY ROBERT HOTCHKIN

God is all about relationship. As a matter of fact, He loves you so much and desires relationship with you so much, He sent His only begotten Son to die on the cross for you. Sometimes we believers are so understandably overwhelmed by the glorious gift of salvation, that we can miss *why* God did what He did at the cross – it is because He loves us and wants relationship with us!

There is no one better at relationship than Him. He is awesome at commitment – promising to never leave or forsake you (Hebrews 13:5). He is amazing at intimacy – always desiring to be near you (James 4:8, Hebrews 4:16). He is really great at giving presents – gifts such as every spiritual blessing in heavenly places (Ephesians 1:3), everything pertaining to life and godliness (2 Peter 1:3), and, of course, the amazing gift of His Son (John 3:16). And wow! is He good at making us feel special –

just think of the number of times that He refers to you as His "beloved" or His "friend" in the thousand-plus page love letter He wrote you in The Bible!

Hands down, there is no one better at relationship than our God. And everyone knows that one of the most important things in creating and maintaining good relationship is good communication. That's why God is always speaking to His people. We just haven't all realized it.

Think of young Samuel in 1 Samuel 3. The Lord keeps calling out to him, but Samuel doesn't realize it. God was speaking to His friend, to His beloved. Samuel *was* hearing God's voice, he just didn't *recognize* that he was hearing God's voice. How many in the church today are similar? How many pine away wishing God would speak to them? How many claim that they never hear God? God is speaking! They are hearing! But like young Samuel they just don't realize it – yet!

Thankfully, Samuel had Eli who came alongside of him, got him to realize that God was speaking to him, and then taught him how to posture himself to hear the Lord (1 Samuel 3:8-9). Samuel listens to the truth that Eli shares with him, chooses to believe by faith that God speaks and that he can hear Him, sets time apart to be with the Lord, and starts a conversation with God that lasts for the rest of his life and launches one of the most powerful prophetic ministries of the Old Testament.

We all need an Eli every once in a while to remind us that God is speaking and that we can hear Him! That's what I love about this book by Patricia King. Like Eli coming alongside of Samuel, in EARS THAT HEAR Patricia comes alongside of you. As you read through the pages of this book, it is like having your very own seasoned mentor teach you how to step into the prophetic. Patricia has more than 30 years of experience as a Christian and prophet, and she shares from that experience to help you learn to clearly hear the voice of God and what He is speaking to you.

In EARS THAT HEAR, Patricia unpacks Scripture to prove to you that God *is* speaking, and that you *can* hear Him. She then teaches you how to tune into His voice and clearly discern it from the voices of the world, the enemy, or your old carnal nature. Plus she gives you simple ways to activate the prophetic anointing in your life.

God is so excited that you picked up this book! He so longs for you to realize that He is speaking to you and that you can hear Him. He has so much he wants to share with you. You know why? Because He is all about relationship and He really, really loves you!

Robert Hotchkin
Christian Services Association / XP

Ears That Hear
By Patricia King

Open my ears, Lord, to hear Your words,

Your heartbeat.

Open my ears to hear You speak

Your ways, Your wisdom.

Open my ears to hear

Your secrets, Your mysteries.

Yes, Open my ears Lord.

Open my ears.

I am listening.

For You.

CHAPTER 1

YOU CAN HEAR!

Jesus said, "My sheep hear My voice" (John 10:27).

Jesus *is* truth and He *only* speaks truth. He has never lied and never will. Therefore, if He said you can hear His voice, you definitely can! So many believers say, "I just can't hear the Lord's voice." Jesus said you do hear Him if you belong to Him, so who is telling the truth? A believer that says they cannot hear? Or Jesus?

Christians hear the voice of God every day but often do not recognize that the voice they hear is the Lord's. They often think what they are hearing comes from their own carnal thoughts, feelings, imaginings, or perhaps even from a deceiving spirit. Others have a false impression that only an elite group of people can actually hear the voice of God and it is not for the ordinary believer. But Jesus said *all* His sheep hear His voice. It is important to learn to identify the clear, unmistaken, voice of God and that is what this book will help you to do.

You *can* hear! You *will* hear!

DISCERNING THE SOURCE

One of the greatest fears in believers is that they are going to hear from a wrong source. We will discuss the various sources of voices in a later chapter, but for now, you can rest confidently in the words of Jesus when He said, "The sheep follow him because they know his voice. A stranger they simply will not follow, but will flee from him, because they do not know the voice of strangers" (John 10:4-5).

While it is important to discern the source of what you are hearing, all too often Christians fear they will hear counterfeit options rather than believing they will easily hear the true voice of God.

GET TO KNOW THE REAL THING

When experts in discerning counterfeit bills are trained, they do not spend time studying the counterfeit, but rather they focus on studying the genuine. Bank personnel who handle true currency every day can easily detect a counterfeit. Studying and experiencing the true is absolutely the best way to detect a counterfeit.

I like fresh cream or half-and-half in my coffee and know it well. When someone pours me a cup of coffee and adds a dairy substitute, I can tell the difference immediately. It is the same with butter. No matter what the substitute, I can tell. Why? Because I use real butter all the time.

If you regularly spend quality time with the Lord, reading and studying His Word, worshipping Him, praying, and intentionally listening for Him to speak, you will learn to easily identify His voice when He speaks. You will have peace within. The more time you spend with Him, the easier it will be to discern the true voice of God. When His voice is familiar to you, you will be able to identify a strange voice immediately.

Ron and I were married in March 1973, so we have lived together as husband and wife for a long time. I can quickly and easily discern Ron's voice, footsteps, breathing, touch, and even the way he opens the door. We have a great deal of traffic through our home. People come and go all the time, but when Ron comes through the door, I know it is my husband even if I cannot see him. This "discernment" has developed through spending lots of time together over many years.

I would never study other men's voices, breathing, footsteps, and touch, in order to better discern Ron's. That would never work and it would only cause confusion. I would never get to know Ron's true voice if I only studied the ways of those who are not Ron. Neither do I worry when my husband speaks to me from the next room thinking, "*Oh no, I wonder if that is Ron? What if I am deceived in thinking that it is Ron's voice but it really isn't?*" No! No! I know Ron's voice and I will not listen to the voice of some other guy if I am waiting to hear from my husband. I know God's voice too. How? In the same way – by spending time with Him and by getting to know Him.

THE NATURE OF GOD'S VOICE

God's voice is holy, righteous, loving, compassionate, merciful, truthful, strong yet gentle, affirming, edifying, peaceful, and kind. His voice can also be authoritative and carry discipline, yet always with love and kindness. His voice is confident yet at rest. His voice will always confirm and support the written Word and will never be contrary to His nature and character.

The fear of hearing from a wrong source (sources such as the carnal flesh or perhaps even a demon) must be overcome. What we fear can come upon us (see Job 3:25). We are to walk in faith and not fear. Jesus shared that if we ask God for something good, He is not going give us evil. He will give us what we ask for because He is a loving Heavenly Father (see Matthew 7:8-10 and Luke 11:12-13). If we ask to hear His voice, He is not going to send us a demonic voice. He Himself will speak to us. We simply need to listen. Oh that our ears would become like satellite dishes and catch everything He says!

GOD LOVES OUR FIRST STEPS

When children learn to walk, they do not simply stand up one day and start walking. They mature through a process of numerous and on-going attempts to establish their balance and eventually walk successfully. Along the way, they might stumble here and there, but the process is delightful. I remember when our grandson took his first steps. He was so cute! He was falling and stumbling all the time for the first month or so, but when he finally learned, you could barely keep up with him. I'm so glad he didn't give up in the beginning of the process. We forwarded emails to everyone with a subject line that said, "KEERAN WALKS." Although he wasn't really walking in a mature way, he was taking a few steps and that filled us with joy.

That is what your Heavenly Father thinks of you when you take your first steps in hearing His voice. Even if you make some mistakes at first, it is simply part of the process and He thinks you're adorable! Maybe you thought He told you to get rid of your "garage" and so you diligently obeyed what you believed was His voice and sold all your stuff in your garage. I can imagine Him chuckling over that and saying to the angels, "Look at my precious child.

He is learning to hear my voice and he thought I said to get rid of his garage. I actually said, 'Get rid of your *grudge*.'" I know the Lord would not be angry over that mistake. He would think it was cute just like you react when you see a little toddler start to walk and take a few falls.

You will hear more and more clearly as you continue to press into Him. The main thing is to believe that you *can* hear!

CHAPTER 2

POSITIONED TO HEAR!

Once you *believe* you can hear, then you can *posture* yourself to hear. God has given you everything you need to enable you to hear His voice, and it is not as complicated as you might think! It is easy!

THE PERSON OF THE HOLY SPIRIT

The Father sent the Helper, the Holy Spirit, to lead and guide you into all truth (see John 16:13). Only the Spirit of God knows the thoughts of God, and you have received "the Spirit who is from God, so that [you] may know the things freely given to [you] by God" (1 Corinthians 2:11-12). Holy Spirit is the Father's gift to you. You cannot earn Him, you simply receive Him as a gift. He will fill you and abide in you. He will awaken your heart to the Scriptures and reveal truth within them to you. He will speak God-thoughts into your heart and give you visions of Kingdom reality and truth. Invite Holy Spirit to fill you and He will. Invite Him to share the mind and heart of God with you and He will. Invite Him to lead and guide you into truth and He will. He is amazing and He is fully committed to you.

THE QUIET TIME

When Moses was leading Israel through the wilderness, he knew the importance of spending time with God. He pitched a tent called The Tent of Meeting away from the camp and met with the Lord every day. When He entered the tent, the pillar of cloud would descend and God would speak face to face with him as a man speaks to a friend (Exodus 33:11).

Mary of Bethany also knew the importance of spending time away from the tasks and assignments of life to be with the Lord. She sat at the feet of Jesus and listened to His Word (see Luke 10:39-42). It is obvious that Mary loved Jesus very deeply. When you are in love, you want to spend time with the one who has captured your heart. You think about them all day long and want to be with them – every waking hour. When people are in love you can tell. They are star-struck. Mary came to know Jesus' heart and ways by sitting quietly and undistracted at His feet. Nothing else captured her attention. Jesus called this "the better part" when Martha challenged her to help her with the preparations.

Like Moses and Mary, you too can spend some time in quiet with the Lord each day. We approach God through faith. Hebrews 11:6 says that "without faith it is impossible to please Him, for he who comes to God must believe that He is and that He is a rewarder of those who seek Him." Still your heart and acknowledge that He is present with you. He is right there. Meditate on that for a few moments and soak in the reality of His presence. What you focus on you empower. There is no set structure that needs to be followed in order to spend time with God. Time with God is motivated by your desire for Him and is led by the Spirit. And we receive extraordinary rewards as we seek Him! There are, however, some components to a devotional time that will help enhance your focus.

PRAISE AND WORSHIP

From a posture of stillness you might like to start praising Him. Ruth Heflin used to say, "Praise Him until the spirit of worship comes. Worship until the glory comes, and then stand in the glory." This is so true. We praise the Lord for all He does. We worship Him for who He is. When you focus on Him and express praise and thanksgiving for all He does, your heart is made glad. Your praise will draw you into intimate adoration, which is called worship, and then you will often actually feel the weight of His presence. This is the glory.

Praise and worship comes from the heart, but sometimes you do not feel like praising. At these times you can simply *choose* to start praising Him. That choice is so important, but sometimes can be difficult. There are many good worship CDs or downloads available today that can help you get focused. Build a worship library and soak in His presence when you can. Praise and worship music in your home, vehicle, or workplace (if permitted) can create an atmosphere of heavenly focus.

I was soaking to some worship music one morning for about an hour and then left the room to get a cup of coffee. When I returned the glory in the room was so thick that I could tangibly feel the presence of the Lord. I had not realized how much glory had manifest by simply soaking and focusing on Jesus. It was glorious!

PRAYER

During your quiet time, share your heart with God. He is interested in everything that pertains to you. He is a great listener and He likes to hear you express your joys and sorrows, and your victories and challenges. He is a relational God. In your prayers, ask Him for all you need. Be bold and confident as you make your requests. He loves to answer your prayers. It is helpful to write down your prayer requests, date them, record any Scripture promise regarding the request, and then record the date of fulfillment and any interesting details or testimonies regarding their fulfillment. Review your prayer journal from time to time, as it will build your faith when you see the record of God's great faithfulness in your life.

LISTENING PRAYER

God does want you to come boldly into His presence and make requests of Him. And He does love answering your prayers. But how would you feel if someone came into your presence and verbally disclosed a list of requests they wanted from you, and then said, "Good-bye" (in prayer we say, "Amen"), and left. We often meet with God in this manner – we don't even take a moment to say, "Hi."

God wants to speak also. Are you listening? He has things to speak to you concerning your requests and your life as well. He also likes to share with you the things that are on His heart. He loves this type of fellowship and interaction with you. He has invited you to be His *friend* as well as His child.

As a young believer I was trained to pray by first taking time to lay down my own thoughts and desires and listen for Him to share His heart with me. Through this posture, I learned to hear God's voice.

THE BIBLE

Hearing the voice of God is easier today because we have the Scriptures available to us. Old Testament characters such as Adam, Abraham, and Noah did not have the written Torah. That came later. The New Testament disciples did not have the gospel or epistles available to them when they were following Christ. We, however, have this advantage today. The words that God spoke to Old and New Testament saints have been written for us to read.

The Bible is a handbook for life and is a powerful way to hear the voice of God. Every time you read the Bible you are hearing God's Word. The Scriptures will keep you in truth and reveal God's heart and ways to you. They will keep your way pure before God and man if you adhere to the truth contained in them.

MEDITATE ON THE SCRIPTURES

Read and meditate on the Scriptures every day. This is the best way to come to know the voice of God. Daily Bible reading is a great discipline for all. Godly disciplines do not save you, but they will truly fortify you. It is the same with physical exercise. If you do not engage in a daily fitness schedule, you will still be born again and you will still be fully loved by God. Your lack of discipline in the realm of physical exercise will not change anything in that sense, but if you don't exercise, you will have limp muscles and a body that will not perform as well as it could. I know this from personal experience! It is the same with spiritual discipline. You will be forever loved and still saved if you never read one verse of Scripture, BUT you will miss the spiritual strength, precision, and engagement with God that you could have if you did.

I like to read at least two to five chapters of the Bible every day. I enjoy reading through a book of the Bible one verse at a time until I am finished with that book. I also like reading from both Old and New Testaments each day. Every time I read, I find certain portions that particularly feed my soul. But even the ones that don't jump off the page at me are still beneficial to read.

As you read your Scriptures, invite the Holy Spirit to highlight meaningful portions to your heart. You will find that the Scriptures He illumines will speak to you in special ways. Hear what He is saying to you. Invite Him to reveal more and more. He will always fill a hungry heart. Jesus said, "The words that I have spoken to you are spirit and are life" (John 6:63). Ponder the verses in addition to any thoughts He gives you that are becoming spirit and life. Then read the Scripture again and again. Still yourself and invite Holy Spirit to inspire you in even deeper ways through that verse. This is called meditating on the Scriptures. It is different from simply reading them and is very powerful as you train yourself to hear the voice of God.

Journal

Keeping track of the insights God speaks to you is helpful for exercising your ability to hear the voice of God. Sometimes I like to write a verse of Scripture into my journal and then ask a particular question of the Lord regarding it. I write down the question and wait quietly for Him to answer. When an answer comes to my thoughts, I write it down. This is one way to cultivate hearing God's voice.

When you journal, you can write expressions of your own thoughts, feelings, and desires as well as what you believe God is saying. You can record your prayer requests, inspiring Scriptures, and the insights God speaks to you. I have published a journal entitled **Sacred Time~Sacred Place.** It includes instruction for having a devotion time, a Bible reading schedule to read through the Bible in a year, and a large section for you to journal your personal times with God (see ordering information at the back of this book). It is enjoyable to go back through your journals and reflect on the promises and insights the Lord gave you.

The more you spend time in the presence of God, the more you will become familiar with His voice. Believe that you can hear His voice. You will! You were created for this purpose.

CHAPTER 3

PREPARING YOURSELF TO HEAR

My father was having a difficult time with his physical hearing a number of years ago. It became so troublesome that he went to the doctor to have his ears checked. After examining him, the doctor said, "You have wax buildup in your ears." The doctor simply extracted the wax and my father's hearing was restored.

In this chapter I'm going to share with you some specific ways you can prepare yourself to hear.

CLEAN THE EARS OF THE HEART

Sometimes there are blocks in our spiritual hearing and we simply need to "get the wax out." The following can block your hearing:

1. **Unconfessed sin.** Sin always puts a separation between you and God and can definitely hinder

your ability to hear God's voice. When you sin, you have listened to the temptations of the enemy and allowed the voice of temptation to trump the voice of God. This causes your hearing to be dull. When you repent from your sin and receive forgiveness, then clarity can come to your hearing. It is like removing "spiritual wax." 1 John 1:9 says, "If we confess our sins, He is faithful and righteous to forgive us our sins and to cleanse us from all unrighteousness."

2. **Listening to ungodly thoughts, words, or sounds.** Your natural ears are gateways to the heart and mind. What you listen to creates systems of belief within you, so beware what you hear. Jesus taught, "Take care what you listen to. By your standard of measure it will be measured to you; and more will be given you besides" (Mark 4:24). He was explaining that what we listen to produces our belief standards in us. The seed of belief produced by what you hear will continue to grow within you. If you listen to truth, then that becomes your standard and more will grow within you.

On the other hand, if you listen to negative and corrupt communication all day long, then that becomes your standard within and more will be added. It is, therefore, extremely important to watch over the ear-gates and guard what enters the heart and mind.

Cleansing the "ear gates" from defiling influences will help us hear clearly the voice of the Lord. The world is full of communication that is disturbing to our spirits. If we fill our hearts and minds with things that are contrary to God's word, then we can be blocked from hearing the true voice of God.

A mother once brought her son to us for ministry as he was experiencing deep depression. We discovered during the ministry that he was listening to some very negative music that was full of hate, rebellion, and even alluded to murder and suicide. After he renounced the music and lyrics, and received forgiveness and deliverance, the depression immediately left him. What we listen to enters our soul. Our minds and beliefs are indeed influenced by what we hear.

Invite the Lord to cleanse your ear-gate from any and all defiling words and thoughts that are contrary to the Word of God. You simply need to ask Him and He will.

3. **Unbelief and doubt.** Some individuals are convinced they cannot hear God and so they don't. Unbelief will clog your spiritual hearing passages.

31

Faith will open them. If you desire to hear from God, then you must believe that you will. James 1:6 says that we "must ask in faith without any doubting." Jesus said that when you pray you are to believe that you receive and you shall have what you requested (Mark 11:24). Jesus also said, "Only believe" (see Luke 8:50). "Only" doesn't leave room for any other option.

Expectation to hear God's voice postures you to hear and is a weapon against unbelief and doubt. Approach the Lord with a joyful expectation to hear from Him. Your expectation opens the way for you to hear.

OVERCOME DISTRACTIONS

My days are extremely busy and my mind is always filled with details, details, and more details. I have learned to shut down and turn off the things that distract me. The following are some things I have personally learned that may help you to overcome distractions.

1. **Find a quiet place.** Whenever possible, find a place that is free from distraction. A quiet place where you can focus and be still before the Lord will help you settle in to spending time in His presence.

2. **Schedule time**. Scheduling time can be beneficial and help you avoid distractions. Once the schedule is set, then guard that time. So often I have scheduled a time but then a phone call comes and someone needs something right away, or I get busy and think, "I will meet with God later." The problem is that the "later" never comes. When the time is set to spend with God, we need to guard that time.

Before Dr. Oral Roberts went on to be with the Lord, I had the privilege of visiting with him. He said that when he went into his prayer time, nothing interrupted him. He guarded what he called his *Sacred Time*. No one was allowed to disturb him or interrupt his time with God in any way – not even his wife and children. He explained that all his days he guarded the sacred time and the sacred place.

3. **Pray in tongues**. If I spend some time praying fervently in tongues before I wait to hear from God, it prepares my spirit and helps me focus on the Lord. The gift of tongues is a wonderful blessing from the Holy Spirit and it is available to every believer. In 1 Corinthians 14, we are taught that when we pray in tongues:

   a. We speak to God (v. 2).

   b. We proclaim God's mysteries (v. 2).

   c. We edify ourselves or build up our spiritual nature (v. 4).

   d. Our spirit prays (v. 14).

4. Decree the Word. Another exercise I engage in to overcome distraction is to proclaim decrees of the Word of God from my book **Decree** (order information is at the back of this book). The decrees are powerful confessions of the Word of God. I like walking up and down in my prayer room making the decrees. It really helps me focus and I feel empowered after I spend some time in proclaiming the Word over my life.

5. Have a notebook to write down random thoughts. Often as believers engage in a time with God, random thoughts invade the focus. These random thoughts might be something like, "Oh, I forgot to pay the utility bill. I need to do that!" or "I better remember to take some meat out the freezer for dinner." Sometimes there are dozens of thoughts like this that come right when you are trying to listen for God's voice. One tool that has helped me over the years (when I remember to utilize it) is to write those things down in a notebook or on a sheet of paper. Then they are out of your thoughts and on paper. You can then deal with those things later and they will not be a distraction to you.

6. **Have your journal, Bible, and study guides at hand.** Have everything you might need close by so that if you are led by the Spirit to engage in a study, you have everything available. Many people use their computers today to engage in on-line Bible research. Remember to avoid the temptation to check email or do something else on the Internet. If you go there you might not get back to your time with God. Believe me, I am speaking from experience!

7. **Read the Scriptures.** As we mentioned earlier, reading the Scriptures is the most powerful way to hear from God. All the Word is awesome, but it is very special when the Holy Spirit highlights certain verses and gives insight. I believe that every time you read the Bible and invite the Holy Spirit to speak with you, He will.

8. **Prayer of Consecration.** God answers prayer that is according to His will. It is His will that you hear from Him. The following is a prayer that covers preparation for hearing His voice.

Heavenly Father,

Open my ears to hear Your voice. I believe You are going to speak to me, so I prepare my heart before You. I ask you to forgive and cleanse me from any and every way I have sinned against you in thought, word, or in deed. In Jesus' name I bind and cast down all distractions and I decree that the voice of a stranger I will not hear. I open my spiritual ears to hear from You alone. Fill me with Your Holy Spirit afresh and speak to me heart. I am listening. Amen.

IDENTIFY YOUR PURPOSE

I remember having the opportunity to meet someone that I really admired. I had longed to personally meet this individual, but when I did, I froze. I did not know what to say. After the initial cordial greetings between us, I was stuck for words. This was the moment I was waiting for yet I had no idea what to say or ask. Outside of having the blessing of meeting them, I had no other purpose. I nervously said something awkward like, "Well, it was nice to meet you," and then walked away, leaving the room. If I had been more aware of the purpose of that visit, I could have prepared questions (I thought of many I could have asked afterwards for sure). I had my moment but went blank. The visit was cut short due to the awkwardness.

Sometimes we are awkward in our times with God because we have not identified the purpose. For example, if the purpose for your time with Him is to have an intimate, heart-to-heart connection, then you will approach Him with a clear intention of sharing your love, worship, and affection, and you will wait for Him to speak His heart in return. This is very different than if you were to approach Him in order to receive some wisdom on a business decision. When you identify your purpose, it will help posture you to hear. If you have purposed to have an intimate time with Him, then you are prepared to hear intimate words from His heart. When a wife shares intimate times alone with her husband, she does not expect to hear words concerning the business of the day within that time. She has an expectation to hear words of love, tenderness, and intimacy.

BE STILL

To hear God, you must listen. Have you ever tried to hear someone speak to you when you are busy performing a task in a room full of people who are all talking? It is very difficult. The best way to listen is to get quiet and focus. Sometimes when I am waiting on God, I deliberately still my thoughts, sit quietly before Him, and wait in a place of rest. Stillness is an important posture for hearing God's voice.

CHAPTER 4

THE WAY GOD SPEAKS

God speaks in diverse ways, and each and every way He speaks is unique and precious. Some people believe that hearing an audible voice is more powerful and carries more authority than the quiet "God-thoughts" He puts in our minds. Others believe that an open vision or trance is a higher level of revelation than the faint images God places in our imagination. Just because something is spectacular does not mean it is the most effective or the most powerful. Jesus, for example, did not have a spectacular entrance into the world, but was birthed in a small stable and laid in a feeding trough for animals. Yet, Jesus is the most authoritative Being in the entire universe. He possesses all authority in heaven and in earth (Matthew 28:18).

It is not the actual *way* God speaks that represents the depth of authority. The actual *purpose* and *influence* of the word are the main factors in the impact of the word. For example, Elijah was a man like us (see James 5:17), yet a very powerful prophet of God in his day who walked in great faith and authority. Scripture reveals a few of the ways Elijah heard from God. God sent an angel to speak to him (see 1 Kings 19 and 2 Kings 1) but one of Elijah's most significant revelations was received through the "still small voice" (1 Kings 19:11-13, KJV). The NIV calls it a "gentle whisper." The influence of the word he received is still influencing masses today. God chose to have the testimony of that encounter placed within Scripture. Even though it was a faint little thought, it carried great power and influence to accomplish God's purpose.

Many believe that if God would just speak to them in an audible voice or send an angel with a message, their faith would be so strong and could then be confident that they heard God speak. This is not actually true.

When Ron and I raised our sons, we only had to speak loud and strong when the boys were not listening or paying attention, or if they were far away. When you are really close to someone, you can hear a whisper. Sometimes the very subtle, still, and faint voice of God will carry the most powerful and significant messages to your heart. The main thing is that you treasure every encounter of hearing the voice of God and embrace each time He speaks as an amazing gift. What a blessing it is to serve a God who speaks in such personal ways to us!

THE STILL, SMALL VOICE

The most predominant way God speaks to His people is through what I call "God-thoughts." This is when He speaks His thoughts into your mind. These thoughts can be identified as coming from God because they completely represent His character and His ways. These thoughts will never violate the counsel of Scripture.

God created your mind so you could reason and communicate. You are created in the image and likeness of God (Genesis 1:27). God has a mind, and therefore, so also do you. Much of your communication with God will be non-verbal expressions that are thought exchanges.

Our minds were created for holy communication and process. It was never God's intention for our minds to be cluttered with sinful and ungodly thoughts. Sinful thought patterns entered us at the fall of man, thus bringing confusion concerning the source of our thoughts. In the beginning our thoughts were perfectly in sync with God's. There were no thoughts in our mind from a sinful or demonic source. We were one with God. We had no need to discern the source of the thoughts within us because we were in complete oneness with God's thoughts. When the serpent came to tempt, he was an outside source. Adam and Eve chose to buy into the lie of the outside voice rather than being true to whom they were before God. Since that time, mankind wrestles with battles in the mind.

Christ is now in our life and has given us a new nature – our spirit man. We are a new creation in Christ. We have the mind of Christ within our born-again nature. The more we focus on this new life and live it out by faith, the more we will be in sync with God's thoughts in our daily experience. In Christ, you have the mind of Christ (1 Corinthians 2:16).

NURTURING YOUR ABILITY TO HEAR THE STILL, SMALL VOICE

Our natural mind needs to be renewed by the Word of God (Romans 12:2). The following are a few ways to nurture your ability to hear God's still small voice.

- Invite the Holy Spirit to reveal any unconfessed sins of the mind. The natural mind is a battlefield and your thoughts determine the course of your life. Proverbs 23:7 says that as you *think* in your heart, so you are. Proverbs We are also encourageds us to "watch over your heart with all diligence, for from it flow the springs of life" (Proverbs 4:23).

- If the Holy Spirit reveals anything to you, then repent (turn away) and ask the Lord to forgive you and to cleanse your mind from all unrighteousness (1 John 1:9).

- Feed your mind with meditations from the Word. Let your natural mind be filled with pure and holy thoughts about God. This will bring renewal to your mind and align it to the mind of Christ. This prepares your conscious mind to hear from God. The more set apart your mind is for God, the more you will be able to identify His voice.

One of the exercises I enjoy is to write a question to God in my journal. You might like to try this simple exercise:

Question: God, how much do you love me?

Now, wait quietly for Him to speak. When you identify a "God-thought," write it down. As I write this paragraph, I am actually engaging in this exercise, and this is what comes to my mind:

(God's Answer): I love you with an everlasting love. My love for you is higher than the highest heaven and deeper than the deepest sea.

After I write down what He spoke to my heart, I meditate on it and thank Him for it. I make sure that it aligns with His loving and righteous character and is confirmed by the Scriptures. Sometimes I will search the Scriptures on the subject I am inquiring about and write down the Scriptures that are quickened by the Spirit.

This type of exercise will season you to hear the voice of God in your thoughts. Make intentional inquiry of Him and wait in quiet expectation for an answer.

THE AUDIBLE VOICE AND SOUNDS

Sometimes God speaks to us through an audible voice or sound. Perhaps you have woken up to an alarm clock or a telephone ring that was audible but realized that the alarm was not set and the phone did not register any calls. Perhaps you have heard your name called.

The audible voice or sounds are one of the ways God can speak to you. Again, I want to emphasize that this is not necessarily more powerful than the still, small voice. Usually God uses this method when He wants to get your undivided attention.

I divide the audible voice and sounds into two categories: outer audible and inner audible. The outer audible voice and sounds are just that. When you hear in this way, your natural hearing perceives the voice just like someone was in the room with you talking. The inner audible is more defined and stronger than the still, small voice, but it is *within* you.

There are many examples in Scripture of the audible voice:

- **Genesis 2:16-17**: God gave Adam instructions to eat of every tree in the Garden of Eden except the tree of knowledge of good and evil.

- **Genesis 3:9**: God called out to Adam and Eve after they had eaten from the tree of knowledge of good and evil.

- **Exodus 3:4**: God called to Moses from the burning bush and told him of His plan to deliver the people of Israel from slavery in Egypt.

- **Exodus 19:9; 20:19-22**: God allowed the people of Israel to hear Him speaking to Moses so that they would believe and follow Moses and fear the LORD.

- **Joshua 1**: God spoke to Joshua to commission him to lead Israel after Moses' death.

- **1 Samuel 3**: While the boy, Samuel, was lying down in the temple where the Ark of the Covenant was, God called to him four times. Samuel thought it was Eli calling for him until Eli told Samuel that it was the voice of God.

- **1 Samuel 23:2**: The Lord spoke to David to attack the Philistines.

- **2 Samuel 7:4-16; Jeremiah 1:4-10; Isaiah 7; Hosea 1**: The word of the Lord came to many prophets to deliver His message to Israel.

- **Matthew 3:16-17**: After Jesus' baptism by John, "a voice out of the heavens said, 'This is My beloved Son, in whom I am well-pleased.'"

- **Matthew 17:1-6**: On the mountain where Jesus was transfigured, Peter, James, and John heard a "voice out of the cloud" say, "This is My beloved Son, with whom I am well-pleased; listen to Him!"

- **John 12:27-29**: While Jesus was telling a crowd about his future death, He prayed, "Father, glorify Your name. Then a voice came out of heaven: 'I have both glorified it, and will glorify it again.'"

- **Acts 9**: On Saul's way to Damascus to arrest Christians, a voice from heaven called out to him saying, "Saul, Saul, why are you persecuting Me?"

- **Revelation 1:9**: John heard a loud voice telling him to write out what he was about to see and send it to the churches.

ANGELIC MESSENGERS

The Bible is also full of accounts where God sends angels with messages to His people. I have always been intrigued by the fact that Mary, mother of Jesus was given the news of her calling to give birth to the Messiah through an angelic messenger. God did not speak to her

Himself through a burning bush or an audible voice, but through an angel.

The following are examples from Scripture of God speaking to people through angels:

- **Genesis 18**: The angel of the Lord appeared to Abraham and Sarah and declared that Sarah would have a son within a year. The angel of the Lord also told Abraham that He was going to Sodom and Gomorrah to see the extent of its wickedness.

- **Judges 6:12**: The angel of the Lord told Gideon that he was a valiant warrior and to deliver Israel from the Midianites.

- **Judges 13**: The angel of the Lord visited both of Samson's parents at different times to tell them of Samson's birth and calling.

- **Daniel 8:15-26; 9:21-27**: Gabriel visited Daniel to give him understanding of a vision of the end of time. Gabriel visited Daniel another time to give him additional insight and understanding.

- **1 Kings 19:5-8; 2 Kings 1**: When Elijah was fleeing from Jezebel, the Angel of the Lord brought Elijah food and told him twice to "Arise and eat." The Angel of the Lord also appeared to Elijah with a message for the king of Israel.

- **Luke 1:11-20**: The angel, Gabriel, appeared to Zacharias with news about the birth of his son, John.

- **Luke 1:26-38**: Gabriel appeared to Mary to let her know that she would be the mother of Jesus and that her relative, Elizabeth, was pregnant with John.

- **Matthew 1:20-22**: An angel appeared to Joseph to encourage him to take Mary as his wife and also gave him the name to call his son, *Jesus*.

- **Luke 2:9-14**: An angel appeared to the shepherd to let them know about the birth of Jesus. A host of angels also appeared praising God and saying, "Glory to God in the highest, And on earth peace among men with whom He is pleased.

- **Matthew 2:13, 19**: An angel appeared twice to Joseph to give him moving directions: first to go to Egypt to escape Herod's murder of all the babies, and then to return to Israel after Herod's death.

- **Matthew 28:1-7**: After Jesus' resurrection, an angel appeared to the women at the tomb to declare that Jesus was no longer dead, and to tell them to notify the disciples of the good news and that Jesus would meet them in Galilee.

- **Acts 8:26**: An angel gave Philip instructions to go and meet an Ethiopian official. Philip was able to explain the Scriptures to the official, lead him to the Lord, and baptize him.

- **Acts 27:23-24**: An angel encouraged Paul not to be afraid because his life, along with the others on the boat, would be saved and he would stand trial before Caesar.

If God chooses to speak to you through an angelic messenger, you are not to worship the angel (Revelation 19:10; 22:9), but turn to the Lord and further process the message with Him. The message the angel brings still needs to be tested like any other word from God. Ask yourself the following questions:

1. Does the word confirm God's character and nature?

2. Is the word confirmed by the Scriptures? (Take into account the whole counsel of God).

3. Does the word witness with your spirit? (Sometimes your mind will not understand but you should have an inner peace.)

4. Does the word bear fruit? (This takes some time to assess.)

5. Does the word come to pass? (This must be given time.)

6. Does the word confirm circumstances in your life?

7. Is the word confirmed by one or two other means? (Matthew 18:16; 1 Timothy 5:19)

8. Does the word draw your attention more towards the Lord or does it distract?

GOD WANTS YOU TO HEAR HIS VOICE

Other ways that God may speak to you include[1]:

- The Holy Spirit – John 16:13; Acts 13:2

- Through peace – Psalms 85:8

- Dreams and visions – Job 33:13-18 (and many examples all throughout Scripture)

- Trances – Acts 10:9-16

- Nature – Psalm 19:1-6; Psalm 29

- A heavenly visitation – 2 Corinthians 12:1-4

- Signs and wonders – Joel 2:30-31

- Confirmation of the message in your spirit by the Holy Spirit – Romans 8:16

- Other people – 2 Peter 1:21; James 5:19-20

- The stories and truths of the Bible – Psalm 119:105;
  2 Timothy 3:16

It's important to remember that God loves you so very much – He is speaking to you and wants you to hear what He's saying! He will choose ways to speak to you that match the unique way He's made you and the message He wants to speak.

In the last chapter we'll look at a few more ways that God speaks to us to give us direction.

[1]This section written using the Study Guide *Receiving and Discerning Revelation* by James W. Goll as a reference.

CHAPTER 5

WORDS FOR LIFE DIRECTION

Life requires that we make many decisions. Every day we make choices on what to eat, what to wear, what to buy, where to go and how to get there, and what activities to engage in. If you have trained yourself to wait for the witness of the Spirit of God before making any minor decision in your day, then weightier decisions like *Whom do I marry? Where do I move? What career do I choose? and What church do I commit to?* it will be much easier to discern the will of God.

THE URIM AND THUMMIM

In the Old Testament we read about the Urim and the Thummim. They signify light and perfection. The Urim and Thummim are a bit of a mystery as there is not too much reference in the Scripture as to what they look like and how the priests used them.

Some scholars believe that they were objects (perhaps small pieces of carved wood or stones) put into some sort of pouch within the breastplate of the priests. It is not clear if they were one object with two sides (one side being the Urim and one side being the Thummin) or two separate objects. It is believed by some that when the priests sought the Lord for a yes or no answer, they would use the Urim and Thummin like casting lots with one representing a yes and the other a no.

Others such as the Talmudic rabbis and Josephus followed the belief that *Urim* meant *lights*, and argued that inquiry of the Lord by Urim and Thummim involved questions being answered by great rays of light shining out of certain jewels on the breastplate.

And yet others believe that when the priests would enter the Holy Place to ask God a question that required a yes or no answer, they would wait for the stones to either light up or not. If they lit up, it was an affirmative answer; if they did not, it was negative.

In any case, today we have the witness of the Spirit within us that gives us peace, assurance, and light within our heart when the Lord speaks affirmation, or a check in our spirit when God is saying no or wants us to pause or stop.

JESUS IS OUR ROCK AND OUR LIGHT

Jesus is our Rock and He is also our Light. He lives in our spirit man by His Spirit. In the same way the priests in the Old Testament waited for light, we can also. This Light illumines our soul from within our spirit and speaks of God's favor and grace on the issue at hand.

I once had a choice to make concerning a direction for our ministry. Someone had offered us a wonderful opportunity, but when I brought it before the Lord, there was no inner witness or "light." (A friend of mine refers to of the positive witness in the spirit as the "green light of grace.") I waited for a couple of days and continued to bring the opportunity before the Lord. In the natural it would have been very beneficial, but there was dullness in my spirit and not light (it felt more like an amber caution light or a red light rather than a green light of clearance). I thought through all the natural blessings that were involved. Everything made sense in my mind, yet there was no witness within. I could not move forward because there was no light on that path. Joy, light, and life filled my soul as soon as I made the official decision to not go in that direction. I had great confidence through the witness within that we were making the right decision, even though it did not make sense to my mind at the time.

On another occasion, I sought the Lord regarding another ministry decision and immediately had "light" fill my heart with a clear witness. I knew immediately to move forward. I have experienced this many times over.

If you need specific direction from God, you can enter His presence by faith and invite Him to illumine your heart with His light and witness. It is not simply a nice feeling or an excitement in the mind, it is a deep peace – a deep witness in your spirit that is deeper than your mind or emotions. It is from His presence within.

THE EXAMPLE OF IGNATIUS

In his writings, *Spiritual Exercises*, Saint Ignatius of Loyola said that before making big decisions, when he didn't have a clear yes or no, he would write out all of the pros and cons for each decision. Then he would take a month and live in the "yes" of a decision. He would act, think, live, and pray as though he had said yes during that time. He then took another month and lived in the "no" of a decision. At the end of two months, he spent a week in prayer and waited for the inner witness of the Spirit in his heart – which decision felt better and bore the most fruit.

I have never spent a month in the *yes*, a month in the *no*, and then another week in prayer, but I have found that sometimes even doing this for a day or so has brought amazing results. Simply ask the Lord to confirm to your spirit the right direction.

As you continue to pray for confirmation on direction and decisions in life, the Lord will bring confirmations from many different directions. The main thing is to look to Him and trust Him alone. Don't try to figure it out in your own mind, but by faith approach Him with intention and focus, and ask for His wisdom, counsel, revelation, and confirmation. He wants to speak, and He will speak.

WARNING

Sometimes others may hear words from the Lord to give to you. This is a blessing indeed; however, you must bring those words to God for your personal confirmation. In particular, be careful of directive words that tell you where to go, what to do, what mate to marry, etc. I am not saying that the Lord will not use others to bring this type of clarity, but you must weigh their words very carefully. Words from others should always bear witness to your spirit and possibly confirm what the Lord has already been speaking to you. Never base a decision on what another claims the Lord has said. You must have your own witness from the Lord.

DIRECTION THROUGH THE SCRIPTURES

I've already shared that reading the Scriptures is the most powerful way to hear from God. As you read, the Holy Spirit will highlight certain verses and bring insight that you've not had before. For example, in the next section I share about a fresh insight into the story of Mary and Martha. I believe that every time you read the Bible and invite the Holy Spirit to speak with you, He will.

The Word of God is "living and active and sharper than any two-edged sword" (Hebrews 4:12). The Scriptures contain direction for life. As you read the Word and study the ways of God outlined in the Scriptures, your direction will be made sure. David declared that God's Word is a "lamp to my feet and a light to my path." 2 Timothy 3:15-17 says that Scripture is "able to give you the wisdom that leads to salvation through faith which is in Christ Jesus. All Scripture is inspired by God and profitable for teaching, for reproof, for correction, for training in righteousness; so that the man of God may be adequate, equipped for every good work." This is awesome! The Bible gives you what you need to come to Christ and be completely prepared for everything God has for you!

LISTEN TO HIM!

Read this story with me:

Six days later Jesus took with Him Peter and James and John his brother, and led them up on a high mountain by themselves. And He was transfigured before them; and His face shone like the sun, and

His garments became as white as light. And behold, Moses and Elijah appeared to them, talking with Him. Peter said to Jesus, "Lord, it is good for us to be here; if You wish, I will make three tabernacles here, one for You, and one for Moses, and one for Elijah." While he was still speaking, a bright cloud overshadowed them, and behold, a voice out of the cloud said, "This is My beloved Son, with whom I am well-pleased; listen to Him!" (Matthew 17:1-5)

Read the last three words that Peter, James, and John heard from heaven: "Listen to Him!" Do you notice the exclamation point? God the Father was trying to drive home a point, and He must have because immediately they fell face down to the ground and were terrified. Just before the voice came, Peter was telling Jesus of his plans to build three shelters for Moses and Elijah (who had come to talk with Jesus) and Jesus Himself. Isn't this just like us? God comes to visit us and we quickly start making plans for the future. The Father's message was clear: **Listen to Jesus**.

Let's look at one more story from Luke 10:38-42:

Now as they were traveling along, He entered a village; and a woman named Martha welcomed Him into her home. She had a sister called Mary, who was seated at the Lord's feet, listening to

His word. But Martha was distracted with all her preparations; and she came up to Him and said, "Lord, do You not care that my sister has left me to do all the serving alone? Then tell her to help me." But the Lord answered and said to her, "Martha, Martha, you are worried and bothered about so many things; but only one thing is necessary, for Mary has chosen the good part, which shall not be taken away from her."

Not too long ago I was rereading this passage and two things jumped out at me.

- Mary sat at Jesus' feet and **listened**. My previous readings focused on Mary just **sitting** at Jesus' feet. While I love to sit at Jesus feet, in a practical sense it can be a challenge to set aside quiet time simply to **sit**, especially with God-given responsibilities and when there is so much that God has put in my heart to **do**.

- When Jesus said, "Martha, Martha," I've always heard "Martha" with a tone of disappointment, like Jesus was shaking his head saying, "Martha Martha, Martha, Martha." This time I heard Jesus saying, "Martha...," but Martha wasn't listening so Jesus said her name again to get her attention because He really wanted to talk with her. Another translation of this passage is "My dear Martha," demonstrating Jesus' great love for Martha.

A quick read of this story shows Martha as busy and distracted, while Mary is devoted and loving. I believe Martha was deeply in love with Jesus but was just expressing it differently through her hard work. But at that moment, the "one thing" that was needed was for her to pause and **listen** just as Mary was listening.

There are times when we need to listen while we sit at Jesus' feet with no other focus but Him. Other times we'll need to be listening as we are about our Father's business. In both cases the message is clear: Listen to Him! Stay tuned into Jesus, listening and responding.

Jesus told His followers:

Everyone who **hears** these words of Mine and **acts** on them, may be compared to a wise man who built his house on the rock. And the rain fell, and the floods came, and the winds blew and slammed against that house; and yet it did not fall, for it had been founded on the rock. Everyone who **hears** these words of Mine and **does not act** on them, will be like a foolish man who built his house on the sand. The rain fell, and the floods came, and the winds blew and slammed against that house;

61

and it fell--and great was its fall (Matthew 7:24-27, emphasis mine).

God is speaking to you and He wants you to hear His voice. Do whatever it takes to get rid of any hindrances that are keeping you from hearing the voice of God clearly and responding to what He says.

Pray this with me:

> *Heavenly Father, I want to know you and I want to hear Your voice more clearly. Thank you that I do hear Your voice because I am a child of God. Forgive me for not paying attention to the many ways you speak to me each day. I want to be one who hears Your words and acts on them so that I can be like one whose house is built upon a rock. Remove every hindrance that keeps me from that which is most important – listening to You and loving You.*

Notes

From Biblestudytools.com

URIM AND THUMMIM

- (Signifying light and perfection)

- In the breastplate (Exodus 28:30; Leviticus 8:8)

- Eleazar to ask counsel for Joshua, after the judgment of Numbers 27:21.

- Only priests could interpret (Deuteronomy 33:8; Ezra 2:63; Nehemiah 7:65)

- Israelites consult (Judges 1:1; Judges 20:18; Judges 20:23)

- Withheld the answer from King Saul (1 Samuel 28:6).

FROM MIRIAM WEBSTER'S ON-LINE DICTIONARY

- Lots thrown to determine God's answers to yes-no questions

Personal Notes

Personal Notes

Personal Notes

Personal Notes

PATRICIA KING

Patricia is president of both Extreme Prophetic and Christian Services Association. She has been a pioneering voice in ministry, with over 30 years of background as a Christian minister in conference speaking, prophetic service, church leadership, and television and radio appearances. Patricia has written numerous books, produced many CDs and DVDs, hosts Extreme Prophetic TV, and is the CEO of a popular online media network – XPmedia.com. Patricia's reputation in the Christian community is world-renowned.

Christian Services Association (CSA) was founded in Canada in 1973 and in the USA in 1984. It is the parent ministry of Extreme Prophetic, a 501(c)(3) founded in 2004 in Arizona. CSA/Extreme Prophetic is located in Maricopa, AZ and Kelowna, B.C. Patricia King and numerous team members equip the body of Christ in the gifts of the Spirit, prophetic ministry, intercession, and evangelism. CSA/ Extreme Prophetic is called to spreading the gospel through

AUTHOR CONTACT INFORMATION

Extreme Prophetic/CSA
U.S. Ministry Center
P.O. Box 1017
Maricopa, AZ 85139

XP Canada Ministry Center
3054 Springfield Road
Kelowna, B.C. VIX 1A5
CANADA

Telephone: 1-250-765-9286
E-Mail: info@XPmedia.com

You've Been Given Eyes that See!

Do you desire to see into the unseen realm? Are you longing to gaze upon Jesus and His Kingdom? Then you need eyes that see!

Eyes that See will help you lay hold of the spiritual sight that you have been given in Christ. You will see in Scripture that the Lord has opened your eyes, and you will learn simple and practical ways to begin practicing seeing in the Spirit.

Decree the Word!

Decree a thing and it shall be established.

Job 22:28

The Word of God is powerful and it will profoundly influence your life. It does not return void, but accomplishes everything that it is sent to do. Patricia King wrote this book to help believers activate the power of the Word in key areas of their lives, including health, provision, love, glory, blessing, favor, victory, wisdom, family, business, spiritual strength and many others.

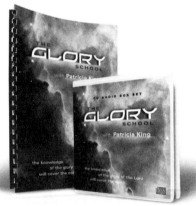

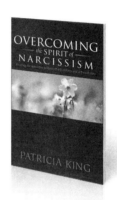
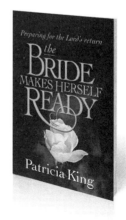

Available at the "Store" at **XPmedia.com.**

The School of Deliverance

8-CD Set and Manual. Do you suffer with guilt, shame, emotional pain, addictive behavior, irrational fears or rejection? Are you trapped by past failures or generational bondage?

This set introduces you to realms of healing and deliverance as Patricia King teaches, preaches, and prophesies you into new-found freedom. Wounds of the past will be healed, and oppressive powers will be broken over lives.

Encountering the Sevenfold Spirit of God

4-CD set by Patricia King. Learn all that the Holy Spirit has for us and how to access it. This teaching is an open door to more wisdom, revelation, understanding, counsel, might, reverence and anointing. Subjects dealt with include: "Who is the Holy Spirit," "The Sevenfold Spirit of God," "The Seven Dimensions," "How to Encounter the Holy Spirit."

Keys to Living in the Glory Realm!

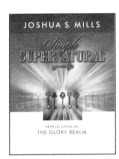

Simple Supernatural. Every believer in Christ is a supernatural being with a supernatural purpose, called to walk in the supernatural ways of heaven while demonstrating God's supernatural Kingdom here on earth!

Joshua Mills shares exciting personal testimonies, biblical keys, and practical guidelines that will launch you into a supernatural lifestyle. Learn how to live in the Glory Realm, win souls supernaturally, manifest God's Word and heal the sick, and more!

Marriage at Its Best!

Supernatural Marriage. Dan Wilson. The key to supernatural marriage is Spirit led intimacy, which makes it possible to successfully enter the extreme and satisfying intimacy of marriage. Man, woman, and God are brought together to create an entity that Satan has no reliable way to attack, no useful battle plan to defeat, and no effective weapon to destroy. A timely and needed message for all married couples!

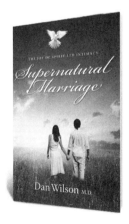

Additional copies of this book
and other book titles from
Patricia King, Extreme Prophetic and XP Publishing
are available at **XPmedia.com**

BULK ORDERS:

We have bulk/wholesale prices for stores and ministries.
Please contact: usaresource@xpmedia.com.

For Canadian bulk orders please contact:
resource@xpmedia.com or call 250-765-9286.

www.XPpublishing.com

**A Ministry of Patricia King and
Christian Services Association**